A TRUE B

D0907564

Women's History in the U.S.

WOMEN
and the
Right to Vote

Cynthia Chin-Lee

Children's Press®
An Imprint of Scholastic Inc.

Content Consultant
Holly Hynson, MA
Department of History
University of Maryland, College Park

Thank you to Elise McMullen-Ciotti for her insights into Indigenous Peoples' history and culture.

A CIP catalog record of this book is available from the Library of Congress.
ISBN 978-0-531-13083-4 (library binding) 978-0-531-13342-2 (paperback)

Scholastic Inc., 557 Broadway, New York, NY 10012

1 2 3 4 5 6 7 8 9 10 R 30 29 28 27 26 25 24 23 22 21

Book produced by 22 MEDIAWORKS, INC.
Book design by Amelia Leon / Fabia Wargin Design

Front cover: The National American Woman Suffrage Association (NAWSA) parade held in Washington, D.C., on March 3, 1913.
Back cover: A suffragette cart advertising "Votes for Women."

Find the Truth

Everything you are about to read is true *except* for one of the sentences on this page.

Which one is **TRUE**?

T or F   In 1917, New York became the first state to grant women the right to vote.

T or F   During the struggle to win the right to vote, more than 90 women spent time in jail.

Find the answers in this book.

Contents

Introduction: A Long Struggle 6

1 The Call for Change

Why did women want voting rights? 8

2 Wins and Losses

What were some of the early successes
of the movement? **20**

A parade for women's suffrage

The **BIG** Truth

Who Opposed Giving Women the Right to Vote?

What groups were against suffrage and why? **28**

Mary Church Terrell

3 The Movement Gains Momentum

How did Elizabeth Cady Stanton, Susan B. Anthony, and others keep the movement going?........30

4 Major Victory

What happened before and after the passage of the Nineteenth Amendment?..............36

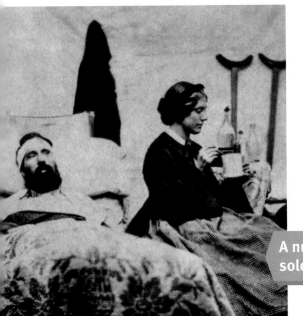

Other Women Who Shaped the Suffrage Movement 42

True Statistics 44

Resources 45

Glossary 46

Index 47

About the Author 48

A nurse takes care of a wounded soldier during the Civil War.

A Long Struggle

American women began demanding suffrage, the **right to vote**, in 1848 at the **women's rights convention in Seneca Falls, New York.** One of the reasons women began demanding rights for themselves was their experience in the **abolition** movement. For decades, women argued that the brutality of slavery must stop. Women also wanted other rights they did not have, like the right to own land and get an education. **Black women also wanted to empower their communities,** oppressed by **racism.**

The battle for women's suffrage had many supporters and lasted many decades. Unlike other fighters throughout history, **women waged a war of words and nonviolent protests.** The movement had setbacks. Many people did not want change, and women's organizations were divided on several issues including race and policy. But there were also victories. **Many women got the right to vote in 1920 when the Nineteenth Amendment was added to the U.S. Constitution.** However, true equal voting rights would take much longer...

Statues at the Women's Rights National Historical Park in Seneca Falls, New York, commemorate women who attended the first women's rights convention in 1848.

Indigenous people, like those shown here in this British representation of the People of the Plains, were not allowed to vote under U.S. law until well into the 20th century.

Before 1776, North American Indigenous Peoples involved both men and women in tribal decisions.

The Call for Change

In 1789, the U.S. Constitution gave the state governments, not the **federal** government, the power to decide who could vote. Most states gave this right to white, land-owning men. Slowly the right to vote was granted to white men without land. In New Jersey, white, land-owning women voted until 1807, when that right was **revoked**. This meant that most people—white women, Indigenous people, and people of color—had no voice in passing the laws they lived under.

Most women were expected to stay home in the 1700s and 1800s. Most families did not send girls to school and most jobs were not open to women.

Women's Lives

In the 1700s and 1800s, women were not expected to take part in politics. Their job was caring for the home and children. This was not easy work. Women had to cook food, sew and wash clothes, milk the cows, make their own soap and butter, and watch their children. Most Americans had large families with three or more kids.

Someone Else's Property

In the U.S., single women were often controlled by their fathers, who had power over their education and ability to earn money. A woman's husband controlled the family's money and property until 1839, when some laws began to change. The lives of enslaved women were far worse. They were often forced to do hard labor. Enslaved people could be beaten if they did not obey their owners. A slave owner could separate an enslaved woman from her children.

Enslaved families had no control of their lives and could be sold at the whim of their owners.

Ending Slavery

In the early 1800s, two sisters from a slave-owning family in South Carolina, Sarah and Angelina Grimké, risked their lives speaking out against slavery. As a result, they were insulted and attacked by mobs. Eventually Sarah Grimké moved north to Pennsylvania and joined the Quakers, a religious group that believes all men and women are equal. The Grimké sisters' involvement in the abolition movement helped form their belief that women needed more rights, including the right to vote.

Angry mobs attacked abolitionists and women's suffrage groups. In 1838, a mob set a fire at an abolitionist meeting at Pennsylvania Hall in Philadelphia.

In 1832, free Black women formed the first women's antislavery society in Massachusetts. One year later, women held their first national convention to talk about how to abolish slavery. Ironically, they debated whether Black women could participate in the convention. They finally agreed to the participation of all women. By 1837, there were 137 women's abolition societies.

In 1833, a Connecticut woman named Prudence Crandall was arrested for teaching Black girls how to read.

13

An Important Friendship

In 1840, Lucretia Mott and Elizabeth Cady Stanton met at an international abolition meeting in London, England. They found themselves seated behind a curtain, excluded from the main meeting room because they were women.

Lucretia Mott

Experiences like this convinced Mott and Stanton that a women's rights movement that was separate from the abolition movement was needed in order for women to make political gains.

Elizabeth Cady Stanton

Seneca Falls

Mott and Stanton returned to the U.S. and in 1848 organized the first women's rights convention in Seneca Falls, New York. The goal was to create a statement outlining the rights of women as citizens of the United States. Stanton penned a "Declaration of Sentiments" based on the Declaration of Independence. It listed 16 issues important for women, including the right to vote, the right to go to college, and the right to own property.

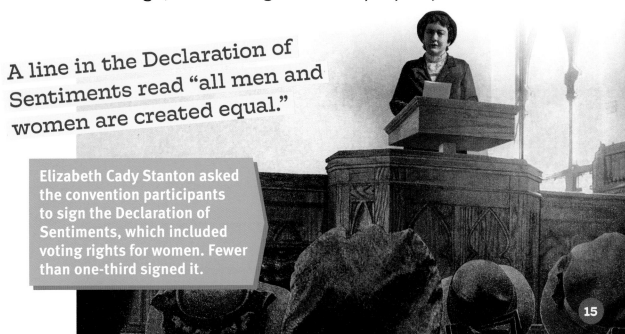

A line in the Declaration of Sentiments read "all men and women are created equal."

Elizabeth Cady Stanton asked the convention participants to sign the Declaration of Sentiments, which included voting rights for women. Fewer than one-third signed it.

Speaking the Truth

After the Seneca Falls conference, women continued organizing conventions. Many prominent free Black women took leadership positions in these conferences. One of them was Sojourner Truth. At the Ohio Women's Rights Convention in

1851, she spoke about the double burden women of color suffered as both enslaved people and as women dominated by men. She also showed the importance of including women of color in the women's rights movement.

Sojourner Truth, a former enslaved woman, gave a speech at the Ohio convention in 1851 known as "Ain't I a Woman?"

Taxation without Representation

Lucy Stone was born in 1818 near Boston, Massachusetts. The eighth of nine children, she grew up to become an abolitionist and a **suffragist.** As a young woman, she worked as a teacher, but spoke out about being paid less than her brother, also a teacher.

Like the colonists during the American Revolution, Stone believed that because she paid taxes, she should have the right to vote. She did not want "taxation without representation." Lucy Stone went on to help found the American Woman Suffrage Association in 1869.

In 1858, Lucy Stone refused to pay her property taxes because she did not have the right to vote. Her home and furniture were taken and sold by the state.

Amelia Bloomer introduced the new style of wearing pants under dresses so women could move more freely. They became known as "bloomers."

In the 1800s women were expected to wear full-length skirts, and pants like these were considered a "scandal."

Women's Suffrage and Temperance

In addition to abolition, many women supported **temperance,** refusing to drink alcohol. Temperance supporters were concerned that drinking could lead to violence, illness, and family problems. Some temperance societies denied women a voice. A temperance leader, Amelia Bloomer, attended the Seneca Falls Convention. In 1851, she introduced Elizabeth Cady Stanton to Susan B. Anthony, who became a key figure in the fight for women's suffrage.

Partners for Suffrage

The daughter of a Quaker abolitionist and temperance supporter, Susan B. Anthony collected names on antislavery **petitions** as a teen. In 1852, she and Elizabeth Cady Stanton founded the Woman's New York State Temperance Society. Anthony dedicated her life to **civil** causes, especially suffrage. She never married or had children. She supported herself and funded suffrage work with the income she made from public speaking.

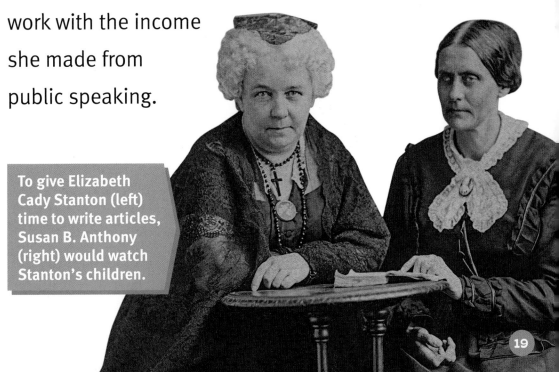

To give Elizabeth Cady Stanton (left) time to write articles, Susan B. Anthony (right) would watch Stanton's children.

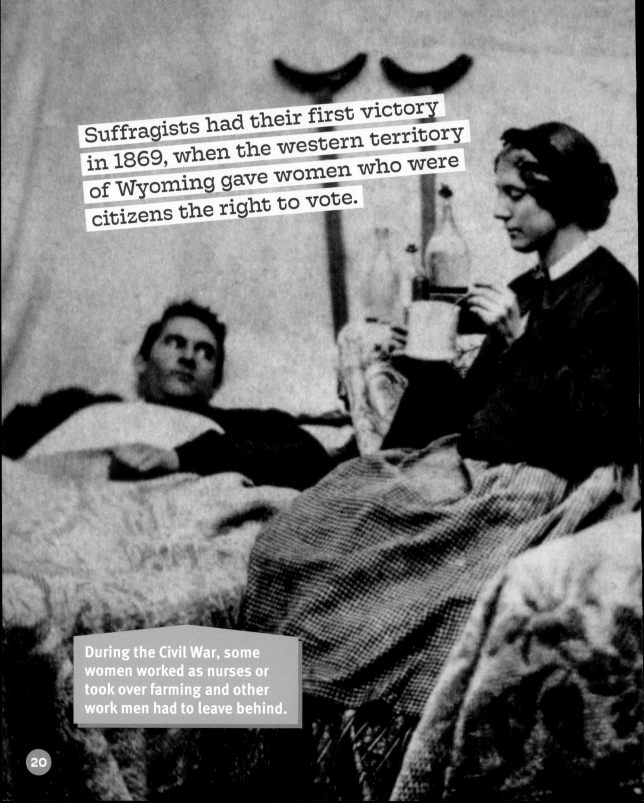

Suffragists had their first victory in 1869, when the western territory of Wyoming gave women who were citizens the right to vote.

During the Civil War, some women worked as nurses or took over farming and other work men had to leave behind.

Wins and Losses

In 1861, the United States was plunged into a bloody civil war as the Southern states **seceded** from the Union over the issue of slavery. Northern women involved in the suffrage movement put aside their fight to work toward abolition. A petition with 400,000 signatures was sent to **Congress**, asking for a constitutional amendment to end slavery. Women also helped the Union in the war effort as nurses, administrators, spies, and workers on farms and in factories.

Back to Suffrage Work

After the Civil War ended in 1865, the Thirteenth Amendment to the Constitution abolished slavery and became the law of the land. Women were now free to continue their fight for suffrage, but postwar divisions in the movement soon appeared. When the Fourteenth Amendment was passed in 1868, it gave all men the right to citizenship but excluded women as citizens. Soon after, the Fifteenth Amendment gave Black men the right to vote, but, again, left women out.

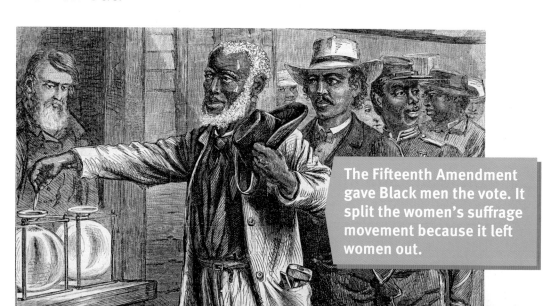

The Fifteenth Amendment gave Black men the vote. It split the women's suffrage movement because it left women out.

Disagreements within the Movement

Women's suffrage leaders disagreed in their support for the new laws. As a result, the suffrage movement split into two main groups. Led by Lucy Stone, the American Woman Suffrage Association supported the Fifteenth Amendment. The National Woman Suffrage

Susan B. Anthony was raised in a family committed to the idea that all people deserved equal rights.

Association, founded by Stanton and Anthony after the Civil War, rejected the amendment because it didn't include women. The competition between the two groups prevented some progress in the movement for the next 20 years.

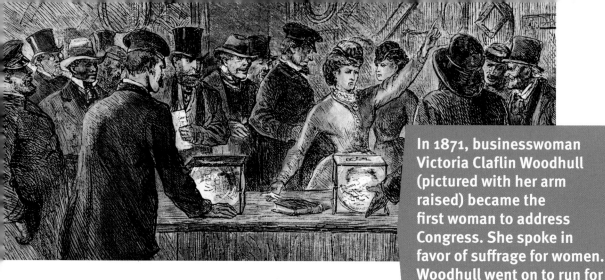

Legal Challenges

Despite this rift, women's groups kept fighting for suffrage in new and creative ways. In addition to protesting taxes, writing articles, publishing newspapers, and signing petitions, women used the courts to challenge the way things were. In 1872, Susan B. Anthony was convicted for trying to vote in Rochester, New York. Her trial brought more attention to the cause.

The Political Equality Association, founded in 1896, promoted women's suffrage.

Changing Views of Women

The Industrial Revolution that began in the mid-1800s brought sweeping change to the U.S. A rise in factory production caused women to join the workforce in large numbers. On Election Day in 1871, more than a hundred Black women in North Carolina disguised themselves as men and went to the polls to vote. Several years later in Wisconsin, 24 female mill workers wrote a statement to the Republican Party insisting that as self-supporting citizens they needed the vote.

The popularity of bicycles in the wake of the Industrial Revolution helped women become more mobile and independent.

The Merge

In 1890, the two major suffrage groups united as the National American Woman Suffrage Association (NAWSA). However, the president of the new group, Carrie Chapman Catt, still favored the vote primarily for white women. She believed Indigenous women should not get suffrage because they might sell their vote. She also believed some immigrants were not educated enough to vote.

The state of Colorado granted voting rights to women in 1893. The state of Idaho followed in 1896.

Carrie Chapman Catt (top left) and Jeannette Rankin (top right) outside the NAWSA office

One of the first Black women to graduate from college, Mary Church Terrell picketed the White House demanding the vote.

Black Suffragists

The National Association of Colored Women (NACW) was formed in 1896 in response to the challenges African American suffragists faced. Sidelined by mostly white suffragist groups, Black women fought for representation for their sex and for their race.

Mary Church Terrell, the daughter of former enslaved parents, was the first president of NACW. She became an activist in the early 1890s, working with Ida B. Wells to fight discrimination and support women's suffrage. Wells was a journalist who investigated lynchings and championed civil rights reforms, including the vote for women.

Ida B. Wells

Who Opposed Giving Women the Right to Vote?

Many groups of people were against women's suffrage for different reasons. Here is why.

Business Owners

Some business owners had a stake in keeping women from voting. Beer makers opposed suffrage because many women supported temperance, and temperance would hurt the sales of beer and other alcoholic drinks. Some factory owners opposed women's suffrage because they were afraid women would support reforms such as laws against using child labor in factories, a common practice at the time.

LIPS THAT TOUCH **LIQUOR** SHALL NEVER **TOUCH MINE!**

Many women supported suffrage because they wanted a reduction in drinking alcohol.

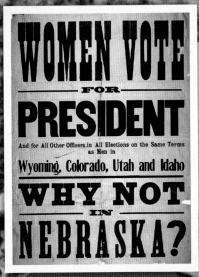

WOMEN VOTE
FOR
PRESIDENT
And for All Other Officers in All Elections on the Same Terms
as Men in
Wyoming, Colorado, Utah and Idaho
WHY NOT
IN
NEBRASKA?

Politicians

Both of the major political parties, the Democrats and the Republicans, were fearful that women's suffrage would be bad for them. After all, if women won the vote, women might vote male politicians out of office. Neither party supported women's suffrage until 1916.

For over 30 years, suffragists fought to get the right to vote in Nebraska. Their efforts finally succeeded in 1919.

MR. SUFFER-YET

BAW-W

Individuals

Some people, both men and women, were afraid that women's right to vote would threaten the traditional roles of women within the family. As early as 1870, anti-suffrage organizations distributed articles, published journals, and spoke publicly about the dangers of giving women the vote.

A cartoon from 1900 expresses a fear that if women got the right to vote, some men would be doing more housework.

Suffragists won attention for the cause by staging marches. The protester seen here carries a box to stand on when giving speeches.

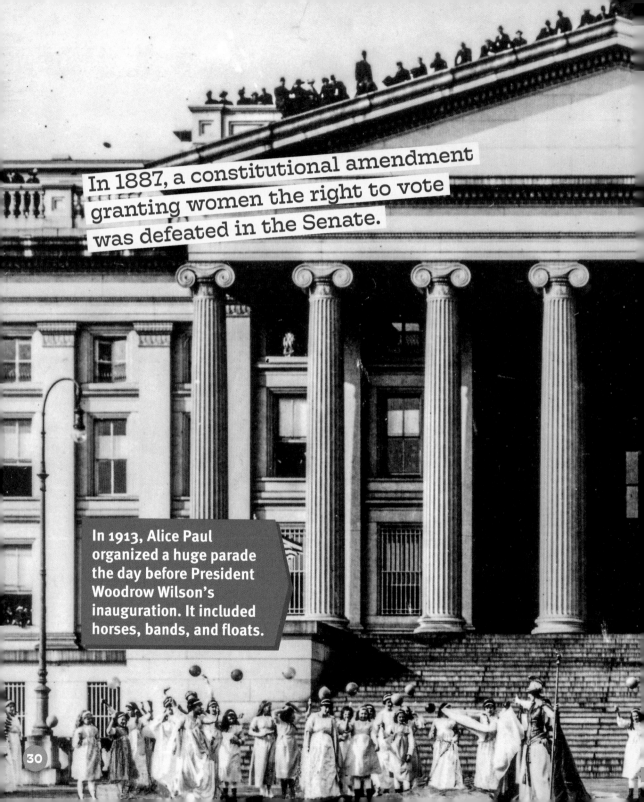

In 1887, a constitutional amendment granting women the right to vote was defeated in the Senate.

In 1913, Alice Paul organized a huge parade the day before President Woodrow Wilson's inauguration. It included horses, bands, and floats.

The Movement Gains Momentum

By 1914, legislation in eight new states, all western, including Washington, California, and Oregon, had granted women the right to vote. Compared to citizens in the East and South, people in western states were more open to women as voters. The western lifestyle encouraged independence. These states wanted to attract outspoken women to settle in the region.

Harriot Stanton Blatch recruited working women to join the suffrage movement.

Second-Generation Leader

Harriot Stanton Blatch, daughter of Elizabeth Cady Stanton, started the Women's Political Union in 1907. In 1912, she planned the first large suffrage parade in New York City, with more than 15,000 people. Blatch reached out beyond the middle- and upper-class women who were the majority of the movement. Marchers included working-class women and laborers from many different backgrounds.

About six hundred men marched for women's suffrage in the 1912 parade in New York City.

Alice Paul

Like Blatch, Alice Paul came from a family with a tradition of public service. In 1907, Paul moved from New Jersey to England and became involved

Alice Paul

with the suffragettes, the name given to the women who were fighting for voting rights in England. There Paul met a fellow American, Lucy Burns, who shared Paul's bold vision of confronting those in politics who sought to deny women the right to vote.

Women fighting for the right to vote used carts like this one to call attention to their cause.

Parade for Suffrage

Returning to the U.S., Paul organized the 1913 Woman Suffrage Procession in Washington, D.C., which attracted half a million people. Black women marched in the parade but were told to march at the back. Refusing to do that, Black activist Ida B. Wells marched with other women from her state. Other women of color also marched, such as Marie Louise Bottineau Baldwin, a Métis woman of the Turtle Mountain Band of Chippewa.

Marie Louise Bottineau Baldwin was the first student from a Native Nation to graduate from the Washington College of Law.

Two-Pronged Approach

In 1915, four eastern states decided not to give women the right to vote. Carrie Chapman Catt, president of NAWSA, had a new idea: She promoted a plan to work for women's suffrage at both the state and

The first woman elected to Congress, Jeannette Rankin organized suffragists in 12 states and helped get suffrage ratified in her home state of Montana.

federal level at the same time. The cooperation between those engaged in these efforts triggered a turning point in the fight for suffrage.

In 1917, suffragists knocked on doors in almost every town and city in New York to gather signatures supporting women's desire to vote.

NATIONAL

Alice Paul rolls out the suffrage flag on August 19, 1920, the day Tennessee became the 36th state to ratify the Nineteenth Amendment.

Major Victory

In 1917, the groups working on state-level suffrage focused on the largest eastern state, New York. Women collected one million signatures in New York, which became the first eastern state to approve voting rights for women. That same year, the U.S. entered World War I, declaring war on Germany. NAWSA, still led by Catt, threw its support behind the war effort. She believed that if women proved their patriotism, it would bolster their claim for voting rights.

Women picketed daily in front of the White House to keep up pressure on President Wilson.

Not everyone agreed with NAWSA's plan. A year earlier, activist Alice Paul had left NAWSA and formed the National Woman's Party. Paul and her team pressured members of Congress and President Woodrow Wilson to support a federal amendment to the U.S. Constitution granting women the right to vote. The National Woman's Party also picketed the White House, enduring rain, snow, and freezing temperatures during the winter of 1917.

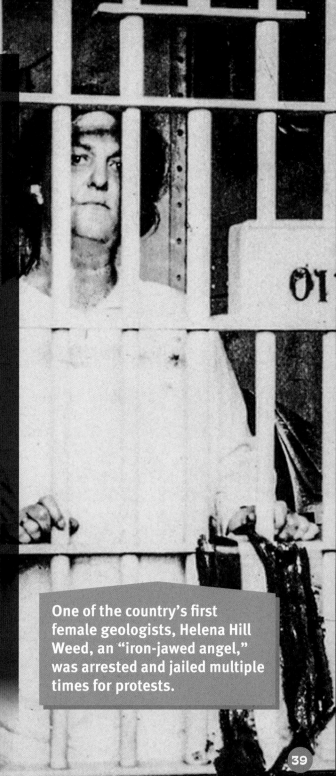

Iron-Jawed Angels

As World War I raged and picketing continued in front of the White House, Paul and about a thousand women protesters were arrested by the police. More than 90 of them were jailed. When the women in jail started a hunger strike, the wardens put them in solitary confinement, beat them, and tried to force them to eat. When the women clenched their mouths closed, the wardens forcibly fed them liquids through the nose. Due to their determination, the women became known as "iron-jawed angels." Accounts of the abuse angered the public and gained sympathy for the cause.

One of the country's first female geologists, Helena Hill Weed, an "iron-jawed angel," was arrested and jailed multiple times for protests.

President Wilson Relents

Realizing that the suffering of the women prisoners made him look cruel, President Wilson finally endorsed the federal amendment granting women the right to vote in January 1918. Congress passed it in the spring of 1919. The Nineteenth Amendment to the Constitution was **ratified** in August 1920. Yet voting rights for all women did not come until later.

Timeline: Women's Suffrage in the U.S.

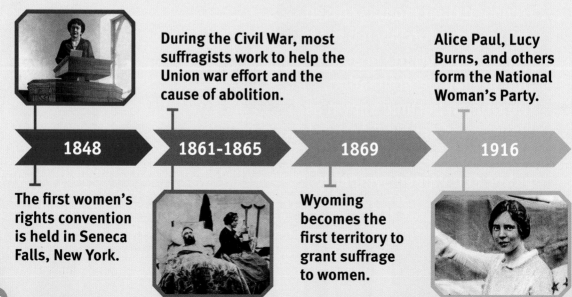

During the Civil War, most suffragists work to help the Union war effort and the cause of abolition.

Alice Paul, Lucy Burns, and others form the National Woman's Party.

1848 — **1861–1865** — **1869** — **1916**

The first women's rights convention is held in Seneca Falls, New York.

Wyoming becomes the first territory to grant suffrage to women.

Progress Continues

In 1924, Indigenous people, including women, finally gained U.S. citizenship with the Indian Citizenship Act. Black women continued to fight against unfair laws that made voting difficult.

Today, while all citizens in the U.S. have the right to vote, activists still work on issues of voters' rights that keep women away from the ballots. 🇺🇸

The Nineteenth Amendment is ratified, making it unlawful to deny the right to vote on the basis of sex.

The Supreme Court bans the poll tax, getting rid of a major barrier to voting for women of color and poor people.

| 1917 | 1920 | 1924 | 1966 |

The U.S. enters World War I. NAWSA supports the war effort in order to gain support for women's suffrage.

The Indian Citizenship Act gives Indigenous people, including women, access to voting. However, most states disregard the new law until the late 1950s.

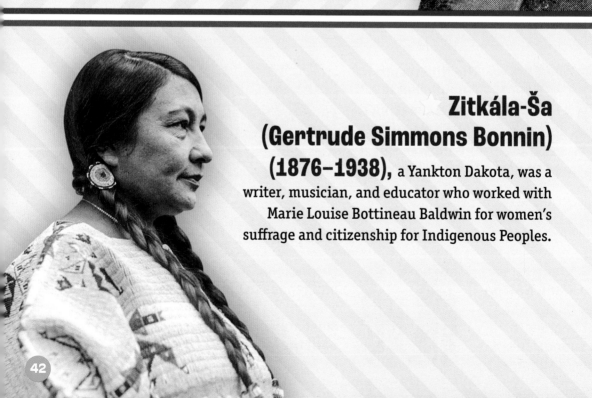

Other Women Who Shaped the Suffrage Movement

Frances E.W. Harper

(1825–1911) became one of the most active Black leaders for suffrage. Her antislavery poetry was a best seller and she helped found the American Woman Suffrage Association.

Zitkála-Ša (Gertrude Simmons Bonnin)

(1876–1938), a Yankton Dakota, was a writer, musician, and educator who worked with Marie Louise Bottineau Baldwin for women's suffrage and citizenship for Indigenous Peoples.

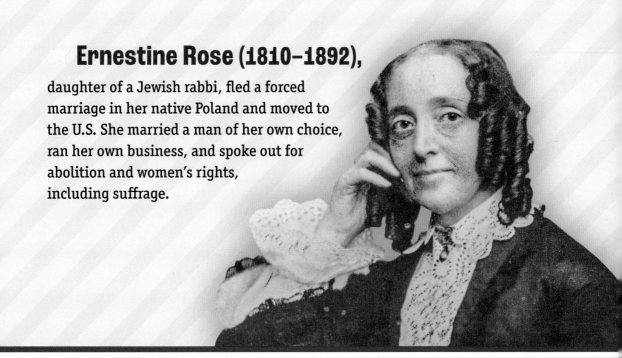

Ernestine Rose (1810–1892),

daughter of a Jewish rabbi, fled a forced marriage in her native Poland and moved to the U.S. She married a man of her own choice, ran her own business, and spoke out for abolition and women's rights, including suffrage.

Mabel Ping-Hua Lee
(1896–1966)
was a Chinese American activist who became involved with women's suffrage when she was just a teenager. In 1912, she rode horseback leading a parade of 10,000 marchers despite not being eligible for citizenship.

Percentage of population with voting rights in 1789: 6 percent (only land-owning white men)

Year of the first women's rights convention: 1848

Year that Wyoming became the first territory to grant suffrage to women: 1869

Number of signatures supporting a federal amendment for women's suffrage collected on a transcontinental road trip in 1915: About 500,000

Number of states that passed women's suffrage laws before the Nineteenth Amendment: 15 (out of 48 states)

Number of states needed to ratify the Nineteenth Amendment: 36 (out of 48)

Number of years it took for women who were citizens to officially get the vote (from the Declaration of Independence until the Nineteenth Amendment): 144 years

Did you find the truth?

F In 1917, New York became the first state to grant women the right to vote.

T During the struggle to win the vote, more than 90 women spent time in jail.

Resources

Further Reading

Brill, Marlene Targ. *Let Women Vote!* Brookfield, CT: Millbrook Press, 1996.

Conkling, Winifred. *Votes for Women! American Suffragists and the Battle for the Ballot.* Chapel Hill, NC: Algonquin, 2018.

Cooney, Robert P.J., Jr. *Winning the Vote: The Triumph of the American Woman Suffrage Movement.* Santa Cruz, CA: American Graphic Press, 2005.

Metz, Lorijo. *The Women's Suffrage Movement.* New York: Rosen Publishing Group, 2014.

Wagner, Sally Roesch, ed. *The Women's Suffrage Movement.* New York: Penguin Books, 2009.

Zimet, Susan, and Todd Hasak-Lowy. *Roses and Radicals: The Epic Story of How American Women Won the Right to Vote.* New York: Viking, 2018.

Other Books in the Series

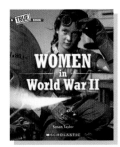

Glossary

abolition (ab-uh-LISH-uhn) the end of the practice of slavery

amendment (uh-MEND-muhnt) a change to the U.S. Constitution

civil (SIV-uhl) of or having to do with the government or people of a country

Congress (KAHNG-gris) the national assembly of U.S. lawmakers

Constitution (kahn-sti-TU-shuhn) the document that establishes the framework of the U.S. government

federal (FED-ur-uhl) referring to the national government as contrasted with state government

petitions (puh-TISH-uhns) formal written requests

poll tax (pohl tax) a tax that must be paid to vote in an election

ratified (RAT-uh-fye-d) approved the passage of a federal or constitutional amendment

revoked (ri-VOKE-d) took away a right, like voting

seceded (si-SEED-id) to formally withdraw from a group or organization

suffrage (SUHF-rij) the right to vote

suffragist (SUFH-ri-jist) a person fighting for suffrage in the U.S.

temperance (TEM-per-ins) moderation or complete abstinence in drinking alcoholic beverages such as beer, wine, and whiskey

Index

Page numbers in **bold** indicate illustrations.

African Americans, 27
Anthony, Susan B., 18–19, **19**, 23, **23,** 24

Baldwin, Marie Louise Bottineau, 34, **34,** 42
Blatch, Harriot Stanton, 32, **32**
Bloomer, Amelia, 18
Burns, Lucy, 33, 40

Catt, Carrie Chapman, 26, **26,** 35, 37
Civil War, 20–21, **20–21,** 22, 23, 40
Crandall, Prudence, **13**

Grimké, Angelina, 12
Grimké, Sarah, 12

Harper, Frances E.W., 42, **42**

Indigenous Peoples and persons, 8, 9, 26, 34, 41, 42

Lee, Mabel Ping-Hua, 43, **43**

Mott, Lucretia, 14–15, **14**

National American Woman Suffrage Association (NAWSA), 26, 35, 37–38, 41
Nineteenth Amendment, 7, 40–41

Paul, Alice, 30, 33, **33,** 34, 36, **36,** 38, 39, 40

Rankin, Jeannette, 26, **26,** 35, **35**
Rose, Ernestine, 43, **43**

Seneca Falls Convention, 6, **6–7,** 15, 18, 40
Stanton, Elizabeth Cady, 14–15, **14-15,** 18–19, **19,** 23, 32
Stone, Lucy, 17, **17,** 23

Terrell, Mary Church, 27, **27**
Truth, Sojourner, 16, **16**

Weed, Helena Hill, 39, **39**
Wells, Ida B., 27, **27,** 34
Woodhull, Victoria Claflin, 24, **24**
World War I, 37, 39, 41

Zitkála-Ša (Gertrude Simmons Bonnin), 42, **42**

About the Author

Cynthia Chin-Lee urges all of us to learn from the suffragists and fight for universal human rights. She has written several books for children including *Operation Marriage* (Reach and Teach) and *Amelia to Zora: Twenty-Six Women Who Changed the World* (Charlesbridge).

Cynthia graduated from Harvard with a degree in East Asian Studies and was an East-West Center Fellow. Born in Washington, D.C., she now lives with her family in the San Francisco Bay area.